Sports Illustrated KIDS

Football
Playbook

SPORTS ILLUSTRATED KIDS BOOKS

Project Editor **Andrea Woo**

Designers **Kirsten Sorton,
Mary Mathieux**

Photo Editor **Annmarie Avila**

Writers **Kiran Gollakota,
Matthew Harrigan, Eric Levenson**

Editors **Justin Tejada,
Sachin Shenolikar**

Copy Editor **Katherine Pradt**

Managing Editor **Bob Der**

Creative Director **Beth Bugler**

Director of Photography
Marguerite Schropp Lucarelli

Imaging **Geoffrey Michaud,
Dan Larkin, Robert Thompson**

TIME HOME ENTERTAINMENT
Publisher **Richard Fraiman**
Vice President, Business Development & Strategy **Steven Sandonato**
Executive Director, Marketing Services **Carol Pittard**
Executive Director, Retail & Special Sales **Tom Mifsud**
Executive Director, New Product Development **Peter Harper**
Director, Bookazine Development & Marketing **Laura Adam**
Publishing Director **Joy Butts**
Finance Director **Glenn Buonocore**
Assistant General Counsel **Helen Wan**
Assistant Director, Special Sales **Ilene Schreider**
Design & Prepress Manager **Anne-Michelle Gallero**
Book Production Manager **Susan Chodakiewicz**
Brand Manager **Allison Parker**
Associate Prepress Manager **Alex Voznesenskiy**
- -
Editorial Director **Stephen Koepp**
- -

SPECIAL THANKS TO: Christine Austin, Jeremy Biloon, Jim Childs,
Rose Cirrincione, Jacqueline Fitzgerald, Carrie Hertan, Christine Font,
Jenna Goldberg, Lauren Hall, Suzanne Janso, Mona Li, Amy Mangus,
Robert Marasco, Kimberly Marshall, Amy Migliaccio, Nina Mistry,
Dave Rozzelle, Adriana Tierno, Vanessa Wu

This page: Jennifer Brown/The Star-Ledger/U.S. PRESSWIRE

Front cover: Damian Strohmeyer (Brady); Robert Beck (Manning);
Al Tielemans (Rodgers); Bob Rosato (Brees); Dusty Cline/Fotolia (balls)

Back cover: (Clockwise) Brad Mangin; Aaron Josefczyk/REUTERS;
Margaret Bowles/AP; Porter Binks; Charles LeClaire/U.S. PRESSWIRE

1 QGD11

Sports Illustrated KIDS
Football
Playbook

New Orleans Saints QB Drew Brees huddles up with his team.

AL TIELEMANS

Contents

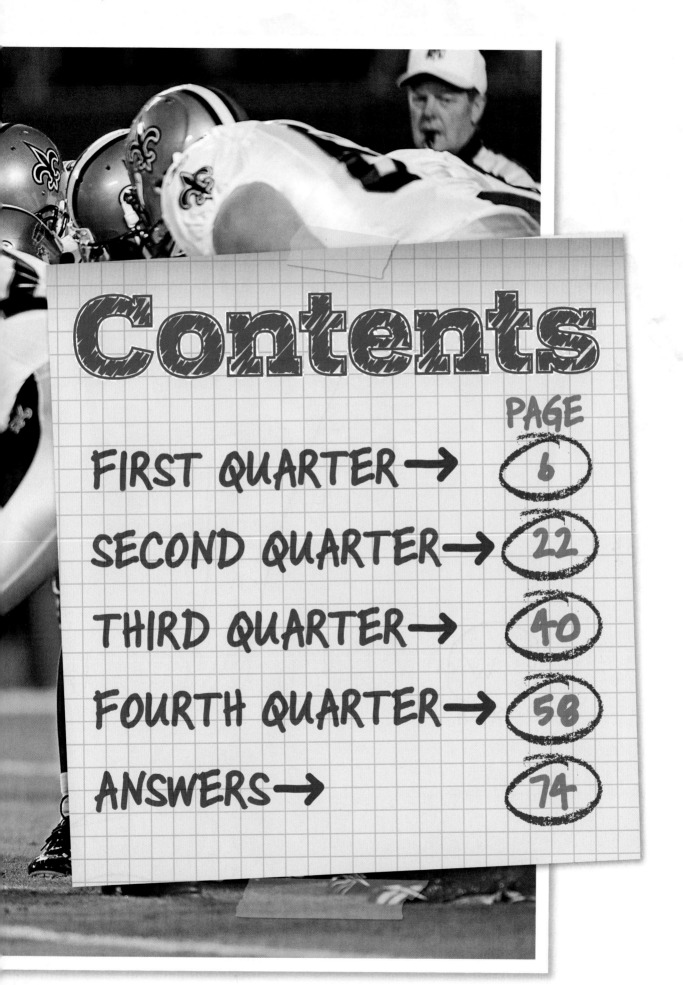

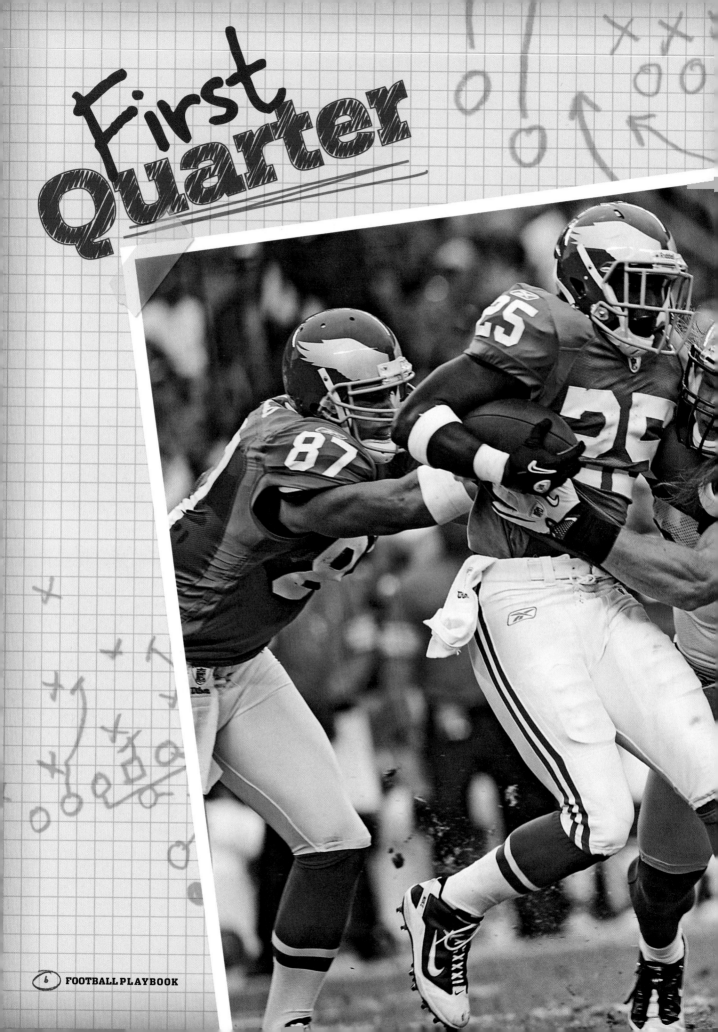

First Quarter

Green Bay Packers linebacker Clay Matthews tries to stop Philadelphia Eagles running back LeSean McCoy from making a big gain.

Funny Photo!

YOUR CAPTIONS: "Watch out here come's that falcon again."

Funny captions from SIKIDS.com:

"Hey, we're the Falcons. Can't we just fly over them?"

"Why am I always the middle of the sandwich?"

"This pillow doesn't feel right."

"This is why I hate Twister."

"Man! I didn't have enough Wheaties this morning!"

GREG NELSON

Find the Open Lane

The names of 12 NFL teams are on the outside of the maze below. But inside the maze are logos of only six of those teams. Pick a team name and follow the maze from the team name to a logo. If you reach a logo, you picked the right team. If you hit a road block, you picked a wrong team.

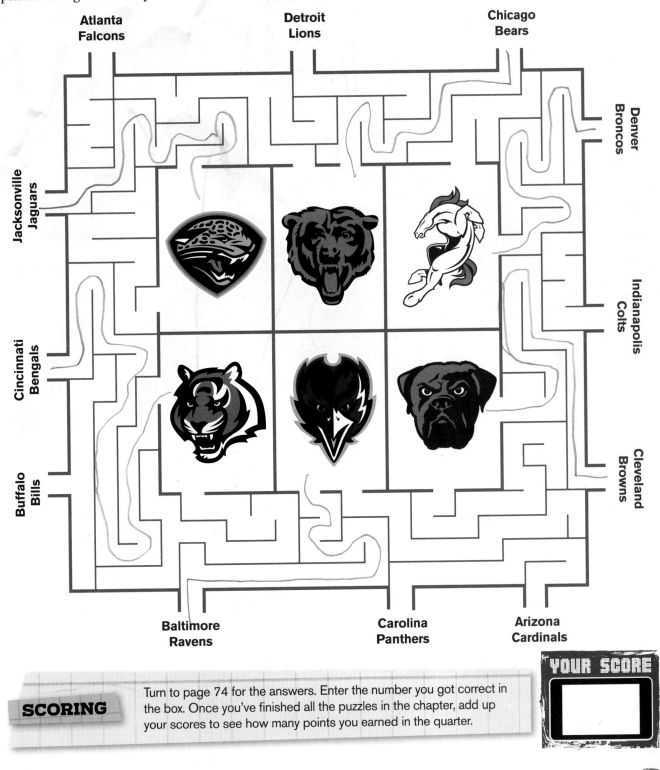

Turn to page 74 for the answers. Enter the number you got correct in the box. Once you've finished all the puzzles in the chapter, add up your scores to see how many points you earned in the quarter.

SCORING

YOUR SCORE

What's in a Name?

Use the letters in the NFL star's name to create new words. See how many words you can come up with! (Each word must be at least three letters long.) We did one for you.

JARED ALLEN

LEADER

ARE

RED

AII

Jar

JARE

SCORING

Count how many words you came up with and then use the key to calculate your points. Once you've finished all the puzzles in the chapter, add up your scores to see how many points you earned in the quarter.

1–5 words = 3 points
6–10 words = 6 points
10–15 words = 9 points
16 or more words = 12 points

DAMIAN STROHMEYER

Guess What I Do

Players may be the stars on the field, but there are many other important jobs in the game of football. See if you can match the job title to the description.

1. Trainer

A. This play-caller manages quarterbacks, running backs, receivers, and linemen.

2. General Manager

B. This medical professional helps injured players recover and keeps healthy players in top physical condition.

3. Defensive Coordinator

C. This coach directs linebackers, cornerbacks, and safeties.

4. Offensive Coordinator

D. This sideline skipper oversees the entire team and makes game-day decisions.

5. Referee

E. The behind-the-scenes brains, this person organizes trades and finds fresh talent to keep the team winning.

6. Head Coach

F. Armed with a flag and a whistle, this striped official enforces the rules on the field.

New York Jets
head coach
Rex Ryan

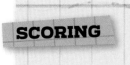

SCORING

Turn to page 74 for the answers. Enter the number you got correct in the box. Once you've finished all the puzzles in the chapter, add up your scores to see how many points you earned in the quarter.

YOUR SCORE

DAMIAN STROHMEYER

Treasure Hunt

Eight pieces of sports equipment that are not related to football are hidden in this photo. Circle the objects that don't belong. Turn to page 74 for the answers. Enter the number you got correct in the box. Once you've finished all the puzzles in the chapter, add up your scores to see how many points you earned in the quarter.

Fake Out

Below are six pairs of helmets. Each pair contains the real helmet used by an NFL team. We made up the logos on the other helmets. Circle the FAKE helmet in each pair.

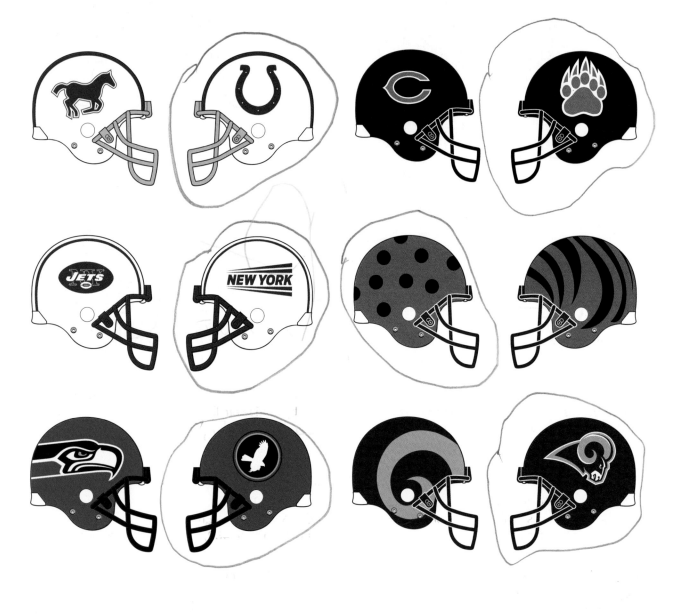

YOUR SCORE

6-6

SCORING

Turn to page 74 for the answers. Enter the number you got correct in the box. Once you've finished all the puzzles in the chapter, add up your scores to see how many points you earned in the quarter.

Mystery Athletes

CLUE #1 The Mystery Athlete was drafted as a catcher by the Montreal Expos in the 18th round of the 1995 Major League Baseball Draft.

CLUE #2 An NFL quarterback, the Mystery Athlete is one of four players in league history to win multiple Super Bowl MVP awards.

CLUE #3 In 2010, the Mystery Athlete set the NFL record for most consecutive pass attempts (335) without an interception.

The Mystery Athlete is:

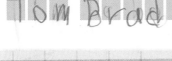
Tom Brady

CLUE #1 The Mystery Athlete played college football at Eastern Illinois University.

CLUE #2 A backup quarterback for his first three NFL seasons, the Mystery Athlete became a starter midway through the 2006 season and has been selected to three Pro Bowls since then.

CLUE #3 The Mystery Athlete holds the Dallas Cowboys' single-season records for passing yards (4,483) and touchdowns (36).

The Mystery Athlete is:

Tony Romo

YOUR SCORE

6-6

SCORING

Turn to page 74 for the answers. Enter the number you got correct in the box. Once you've finished all the puzzles in the chapter, add up your scores to see how many points you earned in the quarter.

The Scrambler

We mixed up the letters in the names of six NFL quarterbacks to make nonsense phrases. Find the player's name by unscrambling each phrase. Use the clues to help you.

1. CUTELY JAR: *Jay Cutler*
Clue: This quarterback led his team to the NFC Championship Game in 2010.

2. RATTY MAN: *Matt Ryan*
Clue: The 2008 Offensive Rookie of the Year has a sure-fire target in wide receiver Roddy White.

3. TARDY MOB: *Tom brady*
Clue: This star has three Super Bowl rings and is one of the best quarterbacks in NFL history.

4. I'M TWO BET: *Tim tebow*
Clue: A Heisman Trophy winner at Florida, this Denver QB is also known for his off-the-field charity work.

5. INNING MEAL: *Eli Manning*
Clue: He has a Super Bowl ring, just like his brother, but one fewer Pro Bowl appearance than his dad.

6. LACK VICE HIM: *Micheal vick*
Clue: A dual threat on the field, this quarterback plays in the city of Brotherly Love.

YOUR SCORE

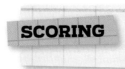
SCORING

Turn to page 74 for the answers. Enter the number you got correct in the box. Once you've finished all the puzzles in the chapter, add up your scores to see how many points you earned in the quarter.

BILL FRAKES

Word Search

See if you can uncover all the football terms listed below. The words are arranged horizontally, vertically, or diagonally, and some are even backward.

Patriots QB Tom Brady gives the ball to running back BenJarvus Green-Ellis.

```
T I N C O M P L E T E X
Z N F I M D E L D D U H
S E T H G I L S Y I W L
A P O A L R F Y R P T I
E K U Q C W O U A R J A
T A C U H K B B M O S P
U S H A D T L G L B V T
O W D C S O I E I O L R
T R O R C H T A A W N E
U V W K A R Z F H L A B
H A N D O F F D W H T G
S E T U C I T H F E I N
```

Hand off
Hail Mary
Fumble
Touchdown
Sack
Shutout
Tackle
Pro Bowl
Blitz
Huddle
Draft
Block
Incomplete

SCORING Turn to page 74 for the answers. Enter the number you got correct in the box. Once you've finished all the puzzles in the chapter, add up your scores to see how many points you earned in the quarter.

YOUR SCORE

Scoring Recap

High-scoring games are fun to watch — but keeping track of the points can be tricky! We took two real games from the 2010 season and noted the scoring activity. Use the key below to add up each team's point total to see if you can figure out the correct score of each game.

Points	
Touchdown	6 points
Field goal	3 points
Safety	2 points
Extra point	1 point
Two-point conversion	2 points

Pittsburgh Steelers	Miami Dolphins
Field goal	Field goal
Touchdown	Field goal
Extra point	Field goal
Touchdown	Touchdown
Extra point	Extra point
Field goal	Field goal
Field goal	Field goal
Total:	**Total:**

St. Louis Rams	Denver Broncos
Touchdown	Touchdown
Extra point	Extra point
Touchdown	Field goal
Extra point	Field goal
Touchdown	Touchdown
Extra point fails	Extra point
Field goal	Touchdown
Field goal	Two-point conversion fails
Touchdown	Touchdown
Extra point	Extra point
Field goal	
Total:	**Total:**

YOUR SCORE

SCORING Turn to page 75 for the answers. Enter the number you got correct in the box. Once you've finished all the puzzles in the chapter, add up your scores to see how many points you earned in the quarter.

Design Your Own Helmet

NFL teams have cool nicknames and great colors. Now here's your chance to design a helmet with your favorite colors!

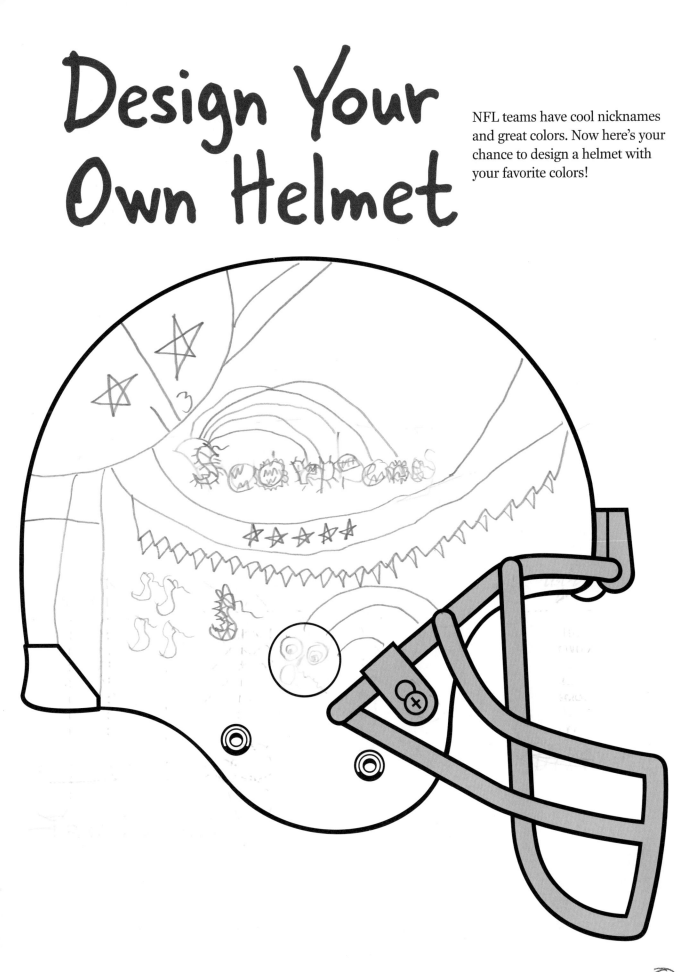

That's My Hair

You never know what you'll find underneath an NFL player's helmet. Match each hairstyle with the football star it belongs to. Write your answers on the lines below.

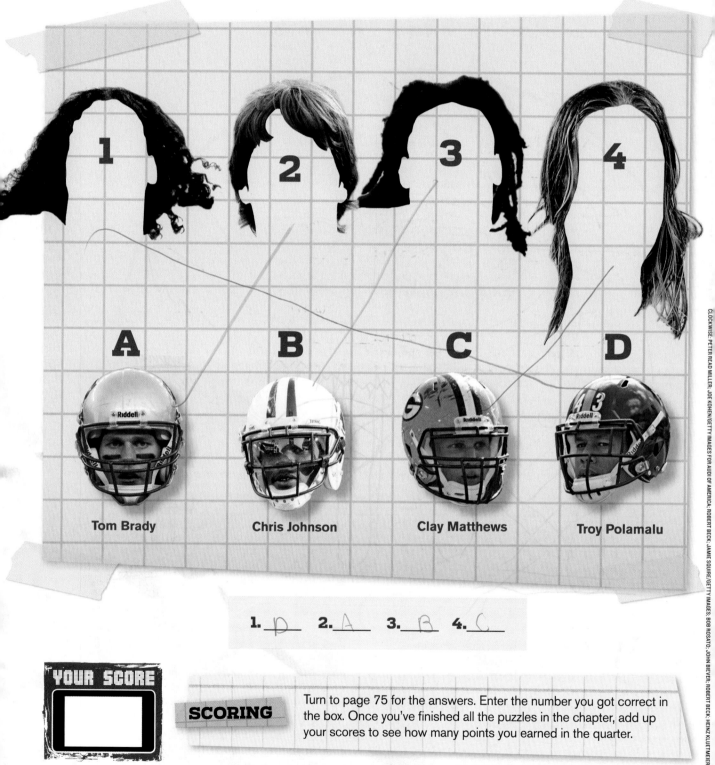

1

2

3

4

A **B** **C** **D**

Tom Brady   Chris Johnson   Clay Matthews   Troy Polamalu

1. D   2. A   3. B   4. C

YOUR SCORE

SCORING Turn to page 75 for the answers. Enter the number you got correct in the box. Once you've finished all the puzzles in the chapter, add up your scores to see how many points you earned in the quarter.

FIRST QUARTER SCORE

Write down your scores for each puzzle below and add up the numbers to find out your total.

Find the Open Lane (p. 9)

Score: 6-6

Fake Out (p. 14)

Score: 6-6

Scoring Recap (p. 18)

Score: 4-4

What's in a Name? (p. 10)

Score: 5

Mystery Athletes (p. 15)

Score: _____

That's My Hair (p. 20)

Score: _____

Guess What I Do (p. 11)

Score: _____

The Scrambler (p. 16)

Score: _____

Total:

Treasure Hunt (p. 12)

Score: _____

Word Search (p. 17)

Score: _____

Extra Point!

See if you can answer this trivia question correctly to convert the extra point. Turn to page 75 for the answer.

How many Super Bowl titles has quarterback Tom Brady helped the New England Patriots win?

A. None   B. One
C. Two   D. Three

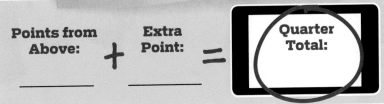

Points from Above: _____ **+** **Extra Point:** _____ **=** **Quarter Total:**

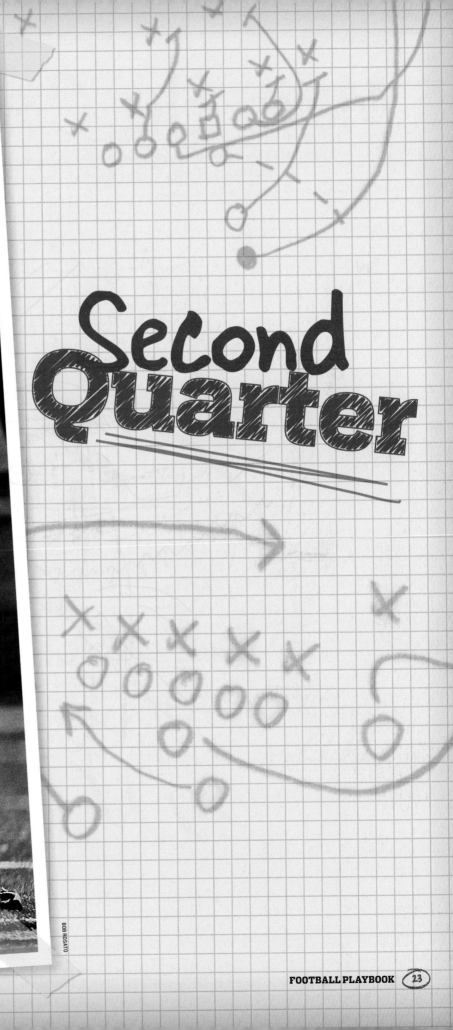

San Diego Chargers quarterback Philip Rivers shouts out a play against the New Orleans Saints.

BOB ROSATO

Second Quarter

Make the Connection

Which NFL team entered the league in 1976 and went 2–26 in its first two seasons?
Connect the dots below to reveal a clue. Turn to page 75 for the answer.

Hint: The NFC team is named after adventurers who roamed the Caribbean Sea.

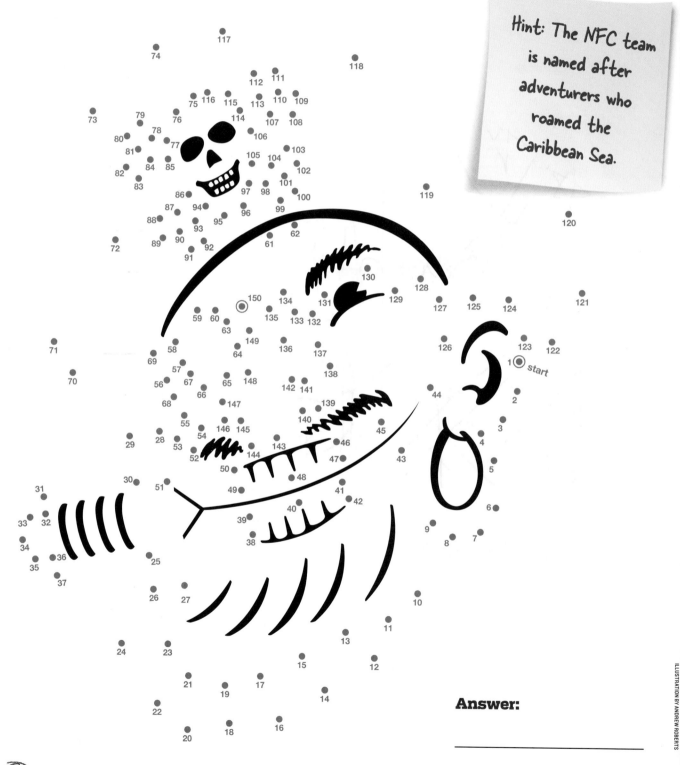

Answer:

ILLUSTRATION BY ANDREW ROBERTS

Funny Photo!

YOUR CAPTIONS:

_____

_____

_____

_____

_____

_____

_____

_____

_____

_____

Funny captions from SIKIDS.com:

"Twilight turned him down, so he joined the Bills."

"Manning will never know what bit him."

"Time to feast on the end zone."

"Oh, I thought you said we played in the AFC Beast."

"Coach said to go for the heart of the offense."

School Days

Have you ever wondered what NFL players were like as kids? We imagined a story, but it's up to you to finish it! First, ask one of your friends to give an answer to each of the categories below. Write all of the answers down, and then read the story aloud. You can play by yourself, too, but be sure not to peek at the story until you're done!

2 + 2 = 4
4 + 4 = 8
8 + 8 = 16
16 + 16 = 32

1. Body part
2. Last night's dinner
3. Famous singer
4. Favorite actress
5. Bird
6. A letter
7. Adjective
8. Verb ending in "s"
9. Animal
10. Your first name
11. Article of clothing
12. Facial expression
13. Piece of jewelry
14. Tech gadget

The NFL is going back to elementary school, and football's best players are seated and ready to learn. The large Ndamukong Suh and Ben Roethlisberger take the desks in the first row.

"Down in front!" Maurice Jones-Drew shouts. "I can't see over your 1._____."

"Come sit over here, Maurice," says Troy Polamalu. "Ray Rice and I were just talking about my mom's

2._____." Polamalu's backpack is covered in 3._____ stickers, and his notebook reads Mr. 4._____.

Rice eyes Jones-Drew's 5._____ sandwich. "I'll trade my 6.__ & __s for that," Rice says.

"No way," Jones-Drew says. "My mom says I won't be big and strong unless I stop eating

7._____ food."

Suddenly, Patrick Willis 8._____ out of his seat. "I just remembered I brought my pet

9._____ 10._____ for show and tell, but I think I left it on the bus!"

"Attention class!" says coach Bill Belichick from the front of the room. "Today we are going to discuss proper sideline behavior. Always wear a cut-off 11._____. Don't be mean to the refs, even if they

12._____ at you. Any questions?"

"How do we get one of those?" asks Larry Fitzgerald, pointing at Belichick's Super Bowl

13._____.

"Oh, these things?" Belichick says. "Hard work, determination, and the best 14._____ money can buy."

Mystery Athletes

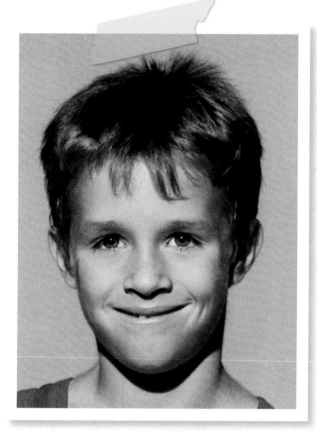

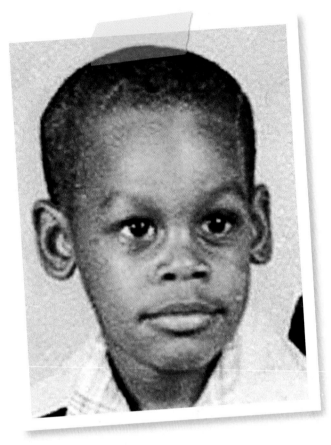

CLUE #1 After four seasons at Purdue University, the Mystery Athlete was chosen by the San Diego Chargers in the second round of the 2001 NFL Draft.

CLUE #2 In 2008, the Mystery Athlete threw for 5,069 yards. It is the second-highest single-season passing total in NFL history.

CLUE #3 The Mystery Athlete was the MVP of Super Bowl XLIV after leading the New Orleans Saints to a 31–17 win over the Indianapolis Colts.

CLUE #1 The Mystery Athlete played both football and basketball at Syracuse University.

CLUE #2 The Mystery Athlete is one of eight players in NFL history with more than 20,000 passing yards and 2,500 rushing yards.

CLUE #3 The 2004 NFC Offensive Player of the Year, the Mystery Athlete led the Philadelphia Eagles to Super Bowl XXXIX. In 2011, he became a quarterback for the Minnesota Vikings.

The Mystery Athlete is:

The Mystery Athlete is:

SCORING Turn to page 75 for the answers. Enter the number you got correct in the box. Once you've finished all the puzzles in the chapter, add up your scores to see how many points you earned in the quarter.

YOUR SCORE

Gridiron Lingo

Football has a lot of funny-sounding words that you might hear only on the field. Test your knowledge of football vocabulary by matching the terms to the definitions.

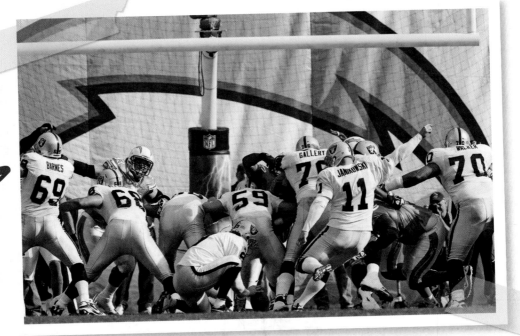

1. PAT

2. Safety

3. Chain gang

4. Pylons

5. Bootleg

6. Dime defense

7. Onside kick

8. Red zone

9. Nose tackle

A. A defensive formation that involves six defensive backs. It is usually used when the defending team is expecting a passing play.

B. The defensive lineman positioned across from the opposing team's center.

C. A score worth two points that occurs when the offensive team's player is tackled in its own end zone.

D. The group of officials who mark off the distance required for a first down.

E. A play in which a quarterback takes the snap and then runs to his left or right before attempting a pass.

F. The area between the opponent's 20-yard line and the goal line.

G. The name for the extra points scored after a touchdown.

H. A play in which the offensive team makes a short kick and then attempts to recover the ball.

I. The orange markers at the four corners of each end zone.

 SCORING Turn to page 75 for the answers. Enter the number you got correct in the box. Once you've finished all the puzzles in the chapter, add up your scores to see how many points you earned in the quarter.

JOHN W. MCDONOUGH

What's in a Name?

Use the letters in the NFL star's name to create new words. See how many words you can come up with! (Each word must be at least three letters long.) We did one for you.

ELI MANNING

IMAGINE
_____
_____
_____
_____
_____
_____
_____
_____
_____
_____
_____
_____
_____
_____
_____
_____
_____
_____

SCORING

Count how many words you came up with and then use the key to calculate your points. Once you've finished all the puzzles in the chapter, add up your scores to see how many points you earned in the

1–5 words = 3 points
6–10 words = 6 points
10–15 words = 9 points
16 or more words = 12 points

YOUR SCORE

What's the Call?

1 Throwing Away the Game?

The New Hampshire Ligers are down by three points and are driving toward the end zone with eight seconds left against the Maine Muskrats. Ligers wide receiver Jeremy Bloss catches a pass over the middle of the field at the Muskrats' 20-yard line. The Ligers are out of timeouts, and Bloss realizes that he won't be able to score a touchdown or get out-of-bounds before time runs out. To try and stop the clock and allow his team to set up for a field goal, Bloss throws the ball behind him to the sideline. You're the referee. Is Bloss's play legal?

2 Out of The Zone

Montana Windmills return man Mason Perry sets up to field a kickoff. The sun is shining bright, causing Perry to misjudge the booming kick. Perry attempts to make the catch while standing on the one-yard line, but the ball hits him on the left shoulder and bounces in the end zone before going out of bounds. You're the referee. Which team gets possession of the ball and where should it be spotted?

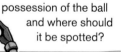

3 Passing Fancy

Quarterback Gerry Singer of the Hawaii Parrots lines up under center and takes a snap in a football game. He hands the ball off to running back DeSean Remston, and then runs a route as a receiver. Remston lofts a pass downfield that is caught by the wide-open Singer. You're the referee. Does the pass count as a completion?

YOUR SCORE

SCORING Turn to page 75 for the answers. Enter the number you got correct in the box. Once you've finished all the puzzles in the chapter, add up your scores to see how many points you earned in the quarter.

Letter Lineup

We've drawn up a football formation using letters instead of X's or O's. Each letter represents an offensive position. (For example, the V is the quarterback.) Fill in the blanks by writing the proper letter above each position to answer this question:

Who holds the NFL record for the most seasons with 1,000 or more rushing yards, and how many seasons did he do it?

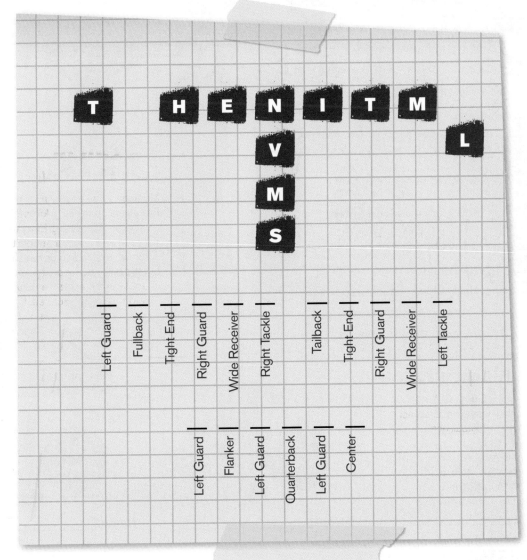

SCORING Turn to page 75 to see if you answered correctly. If it's right, give yourself six points — touchdown! Once you've finished all the puzzles in the chapter, add up your scores to see how many points you earned in the quarter.

Brain Teaser

Shane Lechler, Josh Freeman, and Phil Dawson are part of a skills competition of punting, passing, and kicking. Each player participates in only one event, and trophies are awarded for first, second, and third place.

Josh does not compete in the kicking event and is not a first-place winner.

Shane competes only in punting.

Phil is either the winner of the passing event or places second in one of the other events.

Using the clues above, figure out which event each player participates in, and which trophy each player wins.

1st Place

Name: _____

Event: _____

2nd Place

Name: _____

Event: _____

3rd Place

Name: _____

Event: _____

YOUR SCORE

SCORING

Turn to page 76 for the answers. Enter the number you got correct in the box. Once you've finished all the puzzles in the chapter, add up your scores to see how many points you earned in the quarter.

PETER READ MILLER (LECHLER); CLIFF WELCH/ICON SMI (FREEMAN); TOM CAMMETT/DIAMOND IMAGES/GETTY IMAGES (DAWSON)

Coach Says

Do what the coach says (and only what the coach says) to reveal a fact about running back LaDainian Tomlinson.

1. Coach says, "Cross off all offensive positions listed."
2. Cross off every word with three letters or fewer.
3. Coach says, "Cross off all numbers divisible by three in Row 4 and Column A."
4. Cross off all three-digit numbers.
5. Coach says, "Cross off all the names of Hall of Fame quarterbacks in Row 3 and Column D."
6. Coach says, "Cross off the Olympic sports in Columns B, C, and E."
7. Coach says, "Cross off all words that contain the letter J in Row 2 and Column F."
8. Coach says, "Read the remaining words to learn something about New York Jets running back LaDainian Tomlinson."

	A	B	C	D	E	F
1	Quarterback	Swimming	He	Troy Aikman	Soccer	Adjust
2	9	Holds	Jump	The	NFL	Juggle
3	48	John Elway	Record	For	Running back	Joe Montana
4	Most	Tight end	12	Points	Scored	In
5	A	Bobsled	Diving	Season	Tennis	Center
6	15	Basketball	With	186	Gymnastics	Joke

SCORING Turn to page 76 to see if you got the answer. If it's right, give yourself six points — touchdown! Once you've finished all the puzzles in the chapter, add up your scores to see how many points you earned in the quarter.

YOUR SCORE

Many Faces of Ochocinco

When wide receiver Chad Ochocinco scores a touchdown, he's excited. When he misses a catch, he's frustrated. And when Ochocinco is not sure about a referee's call, he's confused. If you help the frustrated Ochocinco get through the maze, he'll be excited at the end. Use a pen or pencil to make a path that switches back and forth from frustrated Ochocinco to excited Ochocinco. You may move up and down or side to side, but not diagonally. If you run into confused Ochocinco, turn around — you're going in the wrong direction.

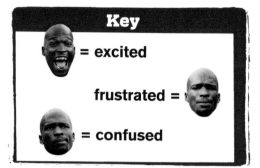

Key

= excited

frustrated =

= confused

START

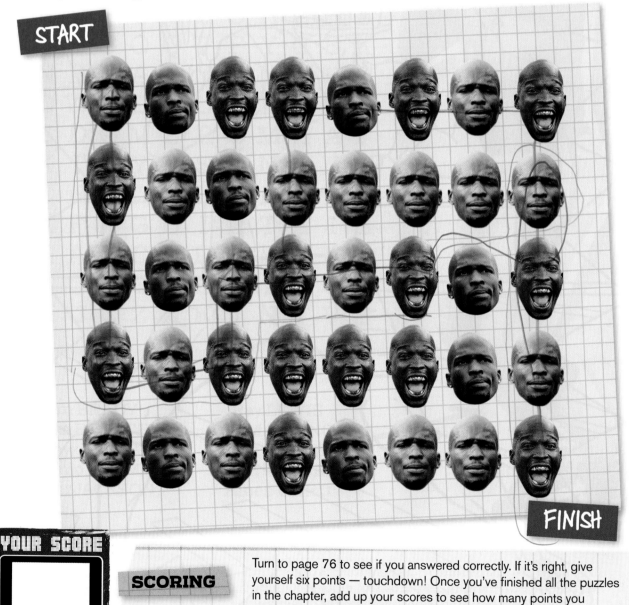

FINISH

YOUR SCORE

SCORING

Turn to page 76 to see if you answered correctly. If it's right, give yourself six points — touchdown! Once you've finished all the puzzles in the chapter, add up your scores to see how many points you earned in the quarter.

No Place Like Home

How well do you know your NFL stadiums and geography? Draw a line from the stadium name to the state it is located in. (It will be one of the states highlighted in blue.) Then draw a line from the state to the logo of the home team that plays there. Use the clues to help you.

Invesco Field at Mile High
The field is located in a city that has an elevation of 5,280 feet.

Heinz Field
Heinz Field's home city has a history of steel manufacturing.

Ralph Wilson Stadium
The stadium is in a city that's famous for chicken wings.

Arrowhead Stadium
Arrowhead resides in a city that shares a name with its neighboring state.

Soldier Field
It's often windy at Soldier Field, which sits on the shores of Lake Michigan.

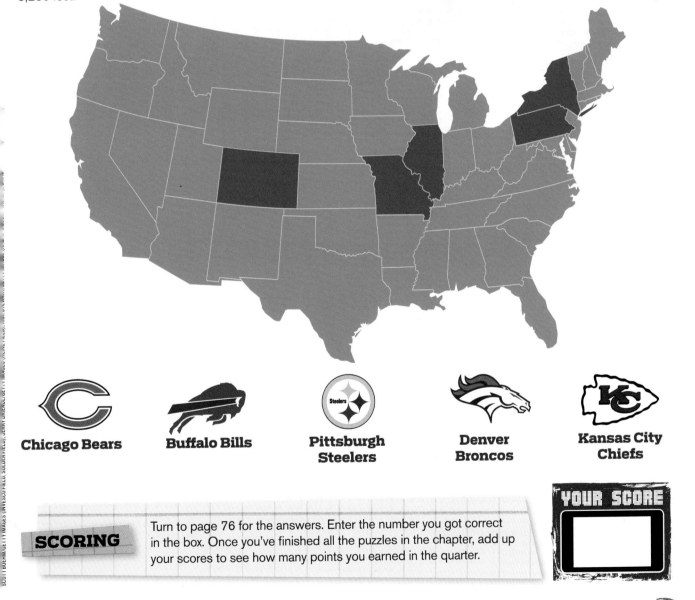

Chicago Bears **Buffalo Bills** **Pittsburgh Steelers** **Denver Broncos** **Kansas City Chiefs**

SCORING — Turn to page 76 for the answers. Enter the number you got correct in the box. Once you've finished all the puzzles in the chapter, add up your scores to see how many points you earned in the quarter.

YOUR SCORE

The Scrambler

We mixed up the letters in the names of six NFL players to make nonsense phrases. Find the player's name by unscrambling each phrase. Use the clues to help you.

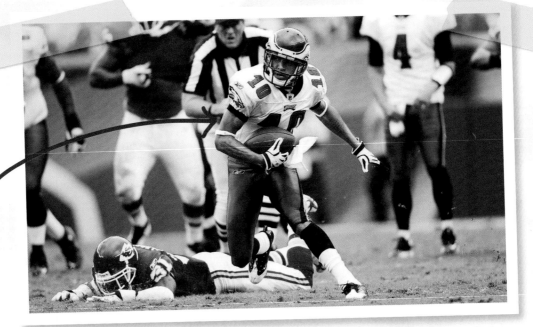

1. JOKE AS SCANNED: __ __ __ __ __ __ __   __ __ __ __ __ __ __

Clue: In 2010, he helped the Eagles complete a miraculous comeback against the Giants by returning a 65-yard punt for the winning touchdown on the final play of the game.

2. CANNOT MEW: __ __ __   __ __ __ __ __ __

Clue: After leading Auburn to the national title in 2011, this QB was taken with the top pick of the NFL draft.

3. ON RAPID EARNEST: __ __ __ __ __ __ __   __ __ __ __ __ __ __ __

Clue: This Vikings running back set the single-game rushing yards record (296) as a rookie in 2007.

4. FRIGHTEN WEEDY: __ __ __ __ __ __ __   __ __ __ __ __

Clue: A six-time Pro Bowler, this defensive end is the Colts' all-time sacks leader.

5. LIZARD TERRY FLAG: __ __ __ __ __   __ __ __ __ __ __ __ __ __ __

Clue: The Arizona wide receiver is known for his touchdown catches and signature dreadlocks.

6. TRAINER AS OF: __ __ __ __ __ __   __ __ __ __ __ __

Clue: In 2010, this Texans running back led the NFL in rushing yards (1,616).

YOUR SCORE

SCORING Turn to page 76 for the answers. Enter the number you got correct in the box. Once you've finished all the puzzles in the chapter, add up your scores to see how many points you earned in the quarter.

SECOND QUARTER SCORE

Write down your scores for each puzzle below and add up the numbers to find out your total.

Mystery Athletes (p. 27)

Score: _____

Gridiron Lingo (p. 28)

Score: _____

What's in a Name? (p. 29)

Score: _____

What's the Call? (p. 30)

Score: _____

Letter Lineup (p. 31)

Score: _____

Brain Teaser (p. 32)

Score: _____

Coach Says (p. 33)

Score: _____

Word Search (p. 34)

Score: _____

Many Faces of Ochocinco (p. 36)

Score: _____

No Place Like Home (p. 37)

Score: _____

The Scrambler (p. 38)

Score: _____

Total:

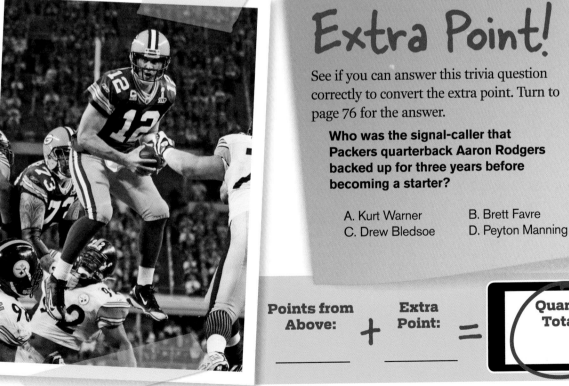

Extra Point!

See if you can answer this trivia question correctly to convert the extra point. Turn to page 76 for the answer.

Who was the signal-caller that Packers quarterback Aaron Rodgers backed up for three years before becoming a starter?

A. Kurt Warner   B. Brett Favre
C. Drew Bledsoe   D. Peyton Manning

Points from Above: _____ **+** **Extra Point:** _____ **=** **Quarter Total:**

PETER READ MILLER

Third Quarter

Dallas Cowboys linebacker DeMarcus Ware goes full speed to try to stuff the San Diego Chargers' offense.

Word Search

See if you can uncover all the football positions listed below. The words are arranged horizontally, vertically, or diagonally, and some are even backward.

```
S T R O N G L J Q T S P
F L Z M P J C O R N E R
Y T E F A S G N O R T S
Y P B L I N E M A N Y T
C E L K C A T E S O N I
G A F Z H W K N T L X G
G U A R D C I A O F D H
C L I F O E N D P S A T
E C R G I N R K E B M E
L S P Z J T M W M O U N
F K I C K E R L Q G U D
P U N T E R J U H E K T
```

Strong safety
Tight end
Wideout
Center
Lineman

Punter
Nose tackle
Corner
Kicker
Guard

**San Diego
Chargers tight end
Antonio Gates**

A Manning Thanksgiving

Want to hear a funny story about the Manning family's Thanksgiving? We imagined a story, but it's up to you to finish it! First, ask one of your friends to give an answer to each of the categories below. Write all of the answers down, and then read the story aloud. You can play by yourself, too, but be sure not to peek at the story below until you're done!

1. Body part
2. Verb ending in "ing"
3. Piece of an NFL uniform
4. NFL team name
5. Animal sounds
6. Color
7. Vegetable
8. Adjective
9. Military weapon
10. Party items
11. Your name
12. Number
13. Any three letters

It's Thanksgiving, and the Manning family is holding a traditional dinner for all of their friends and family.

Archie directs everyone to sit down and takes his spot at the **1.**_____ of the table.

"Where's Eli?" Archie asks, **2.**_____ around the room.

Eli then strolls into the house with his **3.**_____ still on his head. "This food smells

delicious!" he says, "especially the **4.**_____."

As Eli walks toward his seat at the table, Peyton waves his arms and **5.**_____

out a warning to him and others. "Check! Check!" Peyton says. "Watch for **6.**_____

7._____ through the A gap!" All of the guests fill up their plates with turkey, stuffing,

and other **8.**_____ foods.

"Pass the cranberry sauce, bro," Peyton says to his younger brother.

Eli picks up the cranberry sauce and drops back three steps. He throws it with his

9._____ of an arm, and Peyton runs under it and pins the plate against his head. Family

and friends cheer, and **10.**_____ shoot out of the turkey.

"Wow! Nice play, sons," says Archie. "Have you guys been training with **11.**_____?"

"Of course, **11.**_____ is the best!" Peyton says as he gives his dad a big high

12._____.

"Don't play in the house, boys," Mrs. Manning says. "I don't want another mess like when Eli broke

Peyton's **13.**_____ award."

Rushing Ahead

In a 2009 game, which workhorse running back had only eight carries, but finished with 177 yards and two touchdowns after scoring on 80-yard and 79-yard runs? Fill out the answers for the clues below, then read down the highlighted columns to find the answer to the trivia question.

Hall of Famer _____ Rice

A coach calls one of these to stop the clock

Opposite of a loss in yardage

The championship game is the _____ Bowl

A list of 53 players on the team

Nickname of the Colts' city

The tally after a touchdown or a field goal

Last pick in the NFL draft is Mr. _____

Another word for a victory

YOUR SCORE

SCORING

Turn to page 77 to see if you answered correctly. If it's right, give yourself six points — touchdown! Once you've finished all the puzzles in the chapter, add up your scores to see how many points you earned in the quarter.

JOHN W. MCDONOUGH

Funny Photo!

YOUR CAPTIONS:

_____

_____

_____

Funny captions from SIKIDS.com:

"Seahawks fly, don't they?"

"What goes up must come down."

"First down dance!"

"You can't touch this!"

"Bet you can't do super push-ups with one hand."

ROD MAR

NFL Comic Code

Break the code if you want to hear the punch line to the joke below. Match each player listed to the letter on the grid that identifies him by team and position. Then write the letter on the blank line above the player's code number. To get started, we did one for you.

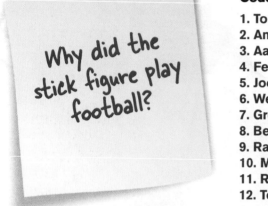

Why did the stick figure play football?

Code Numbers

1. Tom Brady
2. Anquan Boldin
3. Aaron Rodgers
4. Felix Jones
5. Joe Flacco
6. Wes Welker
7. Greg Jennings
8. BenJarvus Green-Ellis
9. Ray Rice
10. Miles Austin
11. Ryan Grant
12. Tony Romo

CODE GRID:

	Patriots	Ravens	Packers	Cowboys
Quarterback	E	B	T	H
Running Back	N	M	W	S
Wide Receiver	L	H	I	A

```
__  __     __  A   __     __  __  __
2   1      11  10  4      3   12  1
```

```
__  __  __  __     __  __  __  __  __  A   __
5   1   4   3      6   7   8   1   9   10  8
```

SCORING

Turn to page 77 to see if you answered correctly. If it's right, give yourself six points — touchdown! Once you've finished all the puzzles in the chapter, add up your scores to see how many points you earned in the quarter.

DAMIAN STROHMEYER

Mystery Athletes

CLUE #1 A five-time Pro Bowl cornerback, the Mystery Athlete tied for the NFL lead in interceptions in 2001. He helped the Tampa Bay Buccaneers defeat the Oakland Raiders in Super Bowl XXXVII.

CLUE #2 The Mystery Athlete is the only player in NFL history to have at least 25 sacks and 40 interceptions in a career.

CLUE #3 The Mystery Athlete has a twin brother who also played in the NFL.

CLUE #1 At the University of Mississippi, the Mystery Athlete set a school record with 86 touchdowns (81 passing, five rushing). He broke the old mark of 56 that was set by his father.

CLUE #2 The Mystery Athlete was the top overall pick of the 2004 NFL Draft.

CLUE #3 The Mystery Athlete was the MVP of Super Bowl XLII. He and his brother are the only siblings to win Super Bowl MVPs.

The Mystery Athlete is:

The Mystery Athlete is:

SCORING Turn to page 77 for the answers. Enter the number you got correct in the box. Once you've finished all the puzzles in the chapter, add up your scores to see how many points you earned in the quarter.

YOUR SCORE

What's in a Name?

Use the letters in the NFL star's name to create new words. See how many words you can come up with! (Each word must be at least three letters long.) We did one for you.

RAY LEWIS

LAWYERS

_____

_____

_____

_____

_____

_____

_____

_____

_____

_____

_____

_____

_____

_____

_____

_____

_____

_____

_____

YOUR SCORE

SCORING

Count how many words you came up with and then use the key to calculate your points. Once you've finished all the puzzles in the chapter, add up your scores to see how many points you earned in the quarter.

1–5 words = 3 points
6–10 words = 6 points
10–15 words = 9 points
16 or more words = 12 points

Sign Language

NFL referees don't just enforce the rules — they also have to remember all the hand gestures that go along with them. See how well you know the signals. Match the call with the signal the ref is making in the picture.

1. _____

2. _____

3. _____

4. _____

5. _____

6. _____

A. Touchdown **B.** Holding **C.** False start **D.** Offside **E.** Delay of game **F.** First down

SCORING Turn to page 77 for the answers. Enter the number you got correct in the box. Once you've finished all the puzzles in the chapter, add up your scores to see how many points you earned in the quarter.

YOUR SCORE

The Scrambler

We mixed up the letters in the names of six NFL quarterbacks to make nonsense phrases.
Find the player's name by unscrambling each phrase. Use the clues to help you.

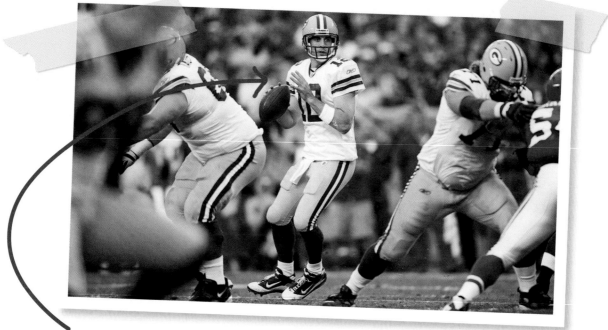

1. A RANGERS ODOR: __ __ __ __ __   __ __ __ __ __ __ __
Clue: This Super Bowl champion had a 101.2 passer rating in 2010.

2. BEST HORRIBLE GREEN: __ __ __   __ __ __ __ __ __ __ __ __ __ __ __
Clue: The Pittsburgh quarterback shares a nickname with the famous clock tower in London.

3. AGENT NINNY MOP: __ __ __ __ __ __   __ __ __ __ __ __ __
Clue: He comes from a family of NFL quarterbacks and holds the record for most MVP awards won (four).

4. SILVER HIP RIP: __ __ __ __ __ __   __ __ __ __ __ __
Clue: A three-time Pro Bowler, he was drafted in 2004 by the Giants, who then traded him to his current team in California.

5. MATCH AS TUB: __ __ __ __   __ __ __ __ __ __
Clue: This gunslinger plays in the Lone Star State and in 2009 led the league in passing yards (4,770).

6. TASTED WARMTH OFF: __ __ __ __ __ __ __   __ __ __ __ __ __ __ __
Clue: The Number One pick of the 2009 NFL Draft, this quarterback leads the charge in the Motor City.

YOUR SCORE

SCORING

Turn to page 77 for the answers. Enter the number you got correct in the box. Once you've finished all the puzzles in the chapter, add up your scores to see how many points you earned in the quarter.

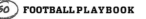

Where's My Teammate?

The names of six pairs of teammates appear in the grid below. Your job is to draw lines that connect each pair. Here's the catch: Lines can pass through empty squares sideways or up and down (not diagonally), and only one line can go through each square. It's harder than it looks! We've done one pair for you.

The grid contains the following names:

- Mark Sanchez
- Matt Ryan
- Vincent Jackson
- Santonio Holmes
- Drew Brees
- Wes Welker
- Philip Rivers
- Peyton Manning
- Roddy White
- Tom Brady
- Reggie Wayne
- Marques Colston

Turn to page 77 to see if you answered correctly.

SCORING

Turn to page 77 to see if you answered correctly.
If it's right, give yourself six points — touchdown! Once you've finished all the puzzles in the chapter, add up your scores to see how many points you earned in the quarter.

YOUR SCORE

ROBERT BECK (SANCHEZ); HEINZ KLUETMEIER (HOLMES)

Athletes in Hiding

The names of football stars are hidden in the sentences below. Can you find them? Use the clues to help you and then underline the name in each sentence. We did one for you.

Blue rice looks disgusting, but it actually is just flavored with berry.

Hint: This safety started all 16 games for the Chiefs as a rookie in 2010.

Answer: Eric Berry

Why did Rod dye his white t-shirt rainbow colors?

Hint: In 2010, this Falcons receiver led the NFL in catches (115) and ranked second in receiving yards (1,389).

Answer: _____

They made Marcus buy a hammer from the hardware store.

Hint: This Cowboys linebacker led the league in sacks in 2008 (20.0) and 2010 (15.5).

Answer: _____

He came and put in some new toner.

Hint: In 2011, this Panthers quarterback became the first rookie to throw for 400 yards in his NFL debut.

Answer: _____

YOUR SCORE

SCORING

Turn to page 77 for the answers. Enter the number you got correct in the box. Once you've finished all the puzzles in the chapter, add up your scores to see how many points you earned in the quarter.

Picture Puzzle

Do these two photographs look the same to you? Look again. The original photo is on top. We made eight changes to the image on the bottom. Time yourself and see how long it takes you to find all eight.

Time Yourself!

_____

SCORE

Out of 8

SCORING

Turn to page 78 for the answers. Enter the number you got correct in the box. Once you've finished all the puzzles in the chapter, add up your scores to see how many points you earned in the quarter.

YOUR SCORE

Running Back Shuffle

Match each NFL running back with the correct trivia fact in the top row and the college he attended.

1 This speedster didn't play for a big-time college program, but he went on to break Marshall Faulk's record of total yards from scrimmage (2,509 in 2009).

2 This pint-sized ball carrier was a first-team All–Pac-10 selection in college. Through 2010, he ranked second behind Fred Taylor on his team's career rushing yardage list.

3 After setting the NFL single-game rushing record in his first year out of a Big 12 school, this bruising running back won the 2007 Offensive Rookie of the Year Award.

4 This dependable player, who was a standout at a Big East school, ranked second on his team in career rushing yards going into the 2011 season.

Adrian Peterson

Chris Johnson

Ray Rice

Maurice Jones-Drew

A UCLA

B Oklahoma

C Rutgers

D East Carolina

YOUR SCORE

SCORING Turn to page 78 for the answers. Enter the number you got correct in the box. Once you've finished all the puzzles in the chapter, add up your scores to see how many points you earned in the quarter.

Just for Kicks

Which NFL kicker has won four Super Bowls and holds the postseason records for most field goals and points? Fill out the answers for the clues below, and then read down the highlighted columns to find the answer to the trivia question.

Avg. is an abbreviation for this word

The home state of the Cardinals

The Mile High city

Player's annual pay

Lions QB _____ Stafford

The first play of a football game

A game official

Another word for a run in football

The _____ of scrimmage

Turn to page 78 to see if you got the answer. If it's right, give yourself six points — touchdown! Once you've finished all the puzzles in the chapter, add up your scores to see how many points you earned in the quarter.

SCORING

YOUR SCORE

DAVID E. KLUTHO

Get the Picture

Each set of pictures below forms the name of a football position. See if you can crack the code and figure out the position each illustration represents. We did one for you.

1. NOSE   GUARD

2. _____   _____

3. _____   _____

4. _____   _____

5. _____   _____

6. _____

THIRD QUARTER SCORE

Write down your scores for each puzzle below and add up the numbers to find out your total.

Word Search (p. 42)

Score: _____

Sign Language (p. 49)

Score: _____

Running Back Shuffle (p. 54)

Score: _____

Rushing Ahead (p. 44)

Score: _____

The Scrambler (p. 50)

Score: _____

Just for Kicks (p. 55)

Score: _____

NFL Comic Code (p. 46)

Score: _____

Where's My Teammate? (p. 51)

Score: _____

Get the Picture (p. 56)

Score: _____

Mystery Athletes (p. 47)

Score: _____

Athletes in Hiding (p. 52)

Score: _____

Total:

What's in a Name? (p. 48)

Score: _____

Picture Puzzle (p. 53)

Score: _____

Extra Point!

See if you can answer this trivia question correctly to convert the extra point. Turn to page 78 for the answer.

Running back Chris Johnson rushed for 2,006 yards in 2009. How many running backs have topped 2,000 yards in one season in NFL history?

A. One   B. Six
C. 11   D. 14

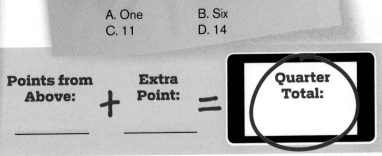

Points from Above: **+** **Extra Point:** **=** **Quarter Total:**

_____   _____

AL TIELEMANS

Jacksonville Jaguars running back Maurice Jones-Drew motors past the Indianapolis Colts defenders.

Fourth Quarter

Funny Photo!

YOUR CAPTIONS:

_____

_____

_____

Funny captions from SIKIDS.com:

"This guy sure wants my autograph."

"Don't leave me! I love you, man!"

"Now this is definitely hanging on by a thread."

"I think I can stretch this into a first down."

"Wait for me!"

ROB CARR/AP

Mirror Image

This masterpiece of Steelers safety Troy Polamalu was left unfinished. It's up to you to complete the work of art. Use the left side as your model.

End Zone to End

SI KIDS

START

Zone

Lead Texans running back Arian Foster on the twisting path to a great touchdown run — but watch out for those fearsome Steelers defenders! (Turn to page 78 for the answer.)

FINISH

SI KIDS

What's the Call?

1 Touch Football

Running back Pablo Jimenez of the Alaska Eagles powers through the line of scrimmage and sprints toward the end zone in a football game against the Portland Suns. Jimenez is far ahead of any Suns defender, but when he reaches the Suns' 20-yard line, he trips over his own feet and falls to the ground. Suns safety Jack Leeder catches up to Jimenez. Leeder knows that if he touches Jimenez while he's on the ground, Jimenez will be ruled down by contact and the Eagles would keep possession. So Leeder carefully takes the ball out of Jimenez's hands without touching any part of his body. Is it now the Suns' ball?

2 Head in the Game

Alabama Plowmen quarterback Emmett O'Lunney has a strong arm, but he's not very accurate. In a game against the rival Georgia Bruins, O'Lunney takes the snap and then fires a pass over the middle that is intended for his favorite receiver, Johnny Certe. But O'Lunney's throw is off target, and it hits an official in the head. The ball bounces in the air and is caught by Alabama tight end Antoine Burgerton. Should this count as a completed pass?

3 Coach's Collision

Star running back Franklin Ripple of the Fairbury Pioneers takes a handoff and bursts through the Lansing Robots' defensive line. He stiff-arms a safety and then dashes down the sideline with nothing but open field in front of him. Robots assistant coach Larry Tan hears the crowd roar, but he can't see the action because his bench players are standing in front of him. Tan leans into the field of play at the Robots' 30-yard line to see what's happening, but collides with Ripple. The impact causes Ripple to stumble out of bounds. Should a penalty be called on Tan?

YOUR SCORE

SCORING

Turn to page 78 for the answers. Enter the number you got correct in the box. Once you've finished all the puzzles in the chapter, add up your scores to see how many points you earned in the quarter.

ILLUSTRATIONS BY SEAN TIFFANY

Super Bowl Sudoku

How many total Super Bowls have NFC East teams won? Solve the sudoku puzzle to find out. Use the letters E, G, H, I, L, N, S, T, and V. Put the nine letters into the boxes so that each letter appears only once in each column, row, and 3×3 box. If you place the letters correctly, the highlighted letters will spell the answer to the question above.

I	V				E	T		
		G	V				S	I
T		S					V	
L	S	I		T				
	G		I		S			
		N			H	I	G	
	L					I		S
V	H			L	I			
		E	T				L	V

Answer:

Turn to page 78 to see if you answered correctly. If it's right, give yourself six points — touchdown! Once you've finished all the puzzles in the chapter, add up your scores to see how many points you earned in the quarter.

SCORING

YOUR SCORE

Word Search

See if you can uncover the last names of the players listed below. Remember, you're just looking for last names. The names are arranged horizontally, vertically, or diagonally, and some are even backward. Once you've circled all the names, write down the letters that are *not* circled on the lines below to find out what the players have in common.

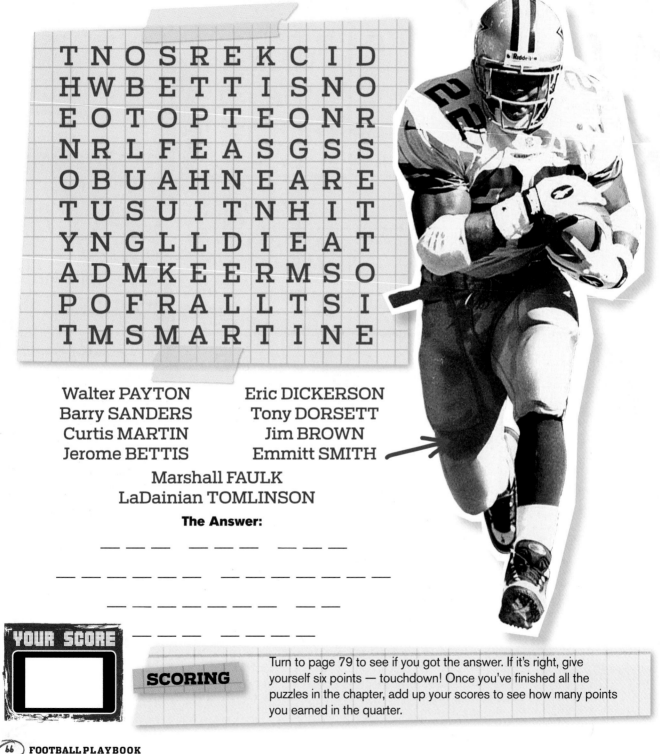

```
T N O S R E K C I D
H W B E T T I S N O
E O T O P T E O N R
N R L F E A S G S S
O B U A H N E A R E
T U S U I T N H I T
Y N G L L D I E A T
A D M K E E R M S O
P O F R A L L T S I
T M S M A R T I N E
```

Walter PAYTON   Eric DICKERSON
Barry SANDERS   Tony DORSETT
Curtis MARTIN   Jim BROWN
Jerome BETTIS   Emmitt SMITH
Marshall FAULK
LaDainian TOMLINSON

The Answer:

_ _ _   _ _ _   _ _ _

_ _ _ _ _ _   _ _ _ _ _

_ _ _ _ _ _ _ _   _ _ _

_ _ _   _ _ _

YOUR SCORE

SCORING

Turn to page 79 to see if you got the answer. If it's right, give yourself six points — touchdown! Once you've finished all the puzzles in the chapter, add up your scores to see how many points you earned in the quarter.

JAMIE SQUIRE/ALLSPORT

Picture Puzzle

Do these two photographs look the same to you? Look again. The original photo is on top. We made eight changes to the image on the bottom. Time yourself and see how long it takes you to find all eight.

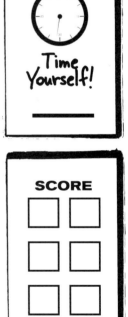

Time Yourself!

_____

SCORE

Out of 8

Turn to page 79 for the answers. Enter the number you got correct in the box. Once you've finished all the puzzles in the chapter, add up your scores to see how many points you earned in the quarter.

SCORING

YOUR SCORE

Don't Trick Me!

Which two-time BCS national champion was one of only two quarterbacks chosen in the first round of the 2010 NFL Draft? To find out, do this true-false puzzle. Decide if the sentence is true or false and circle the letter in that column. (For example, the first sentence is true so we circled the E in the True column.) Then fill in the letter on the line with the same number below to find out the answer.

	True	False
1. At the end of a successful "flea flicker" the quarterback looks to pass to a receiver.	(E)	F
2. Typically, the "Statue of Liberty" is a passing play, not a running play.	J	M
3. In the NFL, a team is allowed to put two quarterbacks on the field during a trick play.	T	L
4. Antwaan Randle El threw a touchdown pass to Hines Ward (left) during a trick play in Super Bowl XL.	O	H
5. LaDainian Tomlinson, a running back, has thrown a touchdown pass in a trick play.	W	N
6. On fourth down, any player may recover a "fumblerooski" — not just the one who fumbled the ball.	B	N
7. It is illegal to fake a spike in the NFL.	D	I

$$\overline{}_{3}\ \overline{}_{7}\ \overline{}_{2}\quad \overline{}_{3}\ \overline{E}_{1}\ \overline{}_{6}\ \overline{}_{4}\ \overline{}_{5}$$

YOUR SCORE

SCORING

Turn to page 79 to see if you answered correctly. If it's right, give yourself six points — touchdown! Once you've finished all the puzzles in the chapter, add up your scores to see how many points you earned in the quarter.

BOB ROSATO

What's in a Name?

Use the letters in the NFL star's name to create new words. See how many words you can come up with! (Each word must be at least three letters long.) We did one for you.

TONY ROMO

<u>MOON</u>

Rom
Root
Tony
Romo
omro
Yoo Yoo

SCORING

Count how many words you came up with and then use the key to calculate your points. Once you've finished all the puzzles in the chapter, add up your scores to see how many points you earned in the quarter.

1–5 words = 3 points
6–10 words = 6 points
10–15 words = 9 points
16 or more words = 12 points

YOUR SCORE

M-V-Pieces

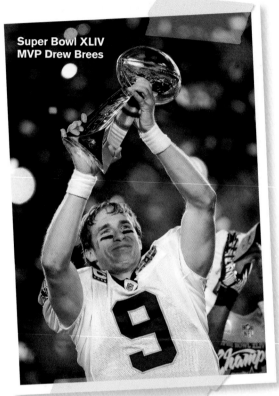

Super Bowl XLIV MVP Drew Brees

Each puzzle piece below contains the name of a Super Bowl Most Valuable Player. Match the name of the player on each piece to the clues in the grid. Then write the letter of the puzzle piece in the space provided below. After you have fit all the pieces into the puzzle, write the letters in order from one through 11 to spell out the name of a person who is not a player but whose name is attached to the award.

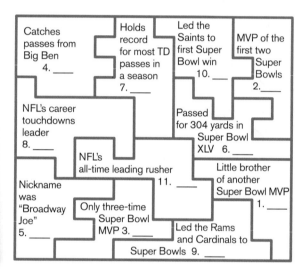

Catches passes from Big Ben 4. ____

Holds record for most TD passes in a season 7. ____

Led the Saints to first Super Bowl win 10. ____

MVP of the first two Super Bowls 2. ____

NFL's career touchdowns leader 8. ____

Passed for 304 yards in Super Bowl XLV 6. ____

NFL's all-time leading rusher 11. ____

Little brother of another Super Bowl MVP 1. ____

Nickname was "Broadway Joe" 5. ____

Only three-time Super Bowl MVP 3. ____

Led the Rams and Cardinals to Super Bowls 9. ____

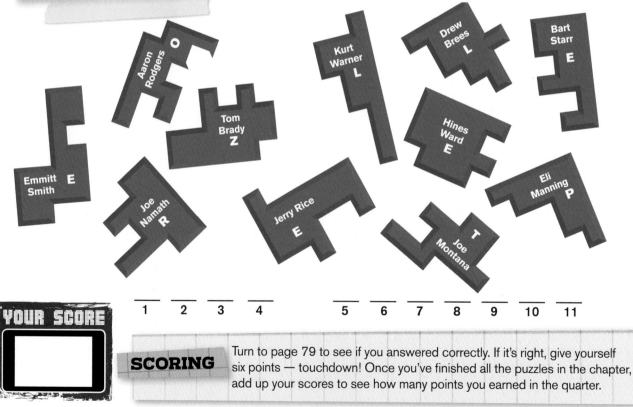

1 2 3 4   5 6 7 8 9 10 11

YOUR SCORE

SCORING Turn to page 79 to see if you answered correctly. If it's right, give yourself six points — touchdown! Once you've finished all the puzzles in the chapter, add up your scores to see how many points you earned in the quarter.

The Scrambler

We mixed up the letters in the names of six NFL players to make nonsense phrases. Find the player's name by unscrambling each phrase. Use the clues to help you.

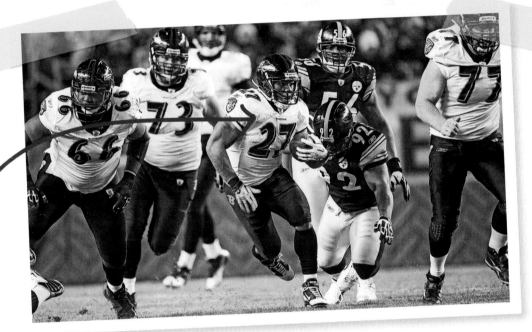

1. RARE ICY: __ __ __ __ __ __ __
Clue: Even though he's small, this running back packs a powerful rushing-receiving punch.

2. WIN DASHER: __ __ __ __ __ __ __ __ __
Clue: He's won two Super Bowl titles with the Steelers and is a TV dance competition champion.

3. GREEN LOGS: __ __ __ __ __ __ __ __ __
Clue: This tight end caught five touchdown passes from Jay Cutler in 2010.

4. CHIRPY RAVEN: __ __ __ __ __ __ __ __ __ __ __
Clue: After winning two national titles in college, this Vikings wideout made his first Pro Bowl in 2009.

5. CZAR HEN MASK: __ __ __ __ __ __ __ __ __ __ __
Clue: A star in the Big Apple, he is one of two quarterbacks in NFL history to play in a conference championship game each of his first two seasons.

6. DESERVE HINT: __ __ __ __ __ __ __ __ __ __ __
Clue: This Bears special teamer holds the NFL record for most touchdown returns in a career (14).

Turn to page 79 for the answers.

SCORING

Turn to page 79 for the answers. Enter the number you got correct in the box. Once you've finished all the puzzles in the chapter, add up your scores to see how many points you earned in the quarter.

YOUR SCORE

Signature Moves

Getting an athlete's signature is one of the coolest things about being a fan. But sometimes the writing is almost impossible to read. See if you can figure out who signed these real athlete autographs. Use the clue to help you. We did the first one.

1. Since bursting onto the NFL scene in 2007, this Vikings running back has made four Pro Bowls.

Adrian Peterson

2. This Texans linebacker was the first pick in the 2006 NFL Draft. He shares a nickname with a famous video game character.

_____

3. After guiding his team to victory in Super Bowl XLIV, this quarterback won the SPORTS ILLUSTRATED Sportsman of the Year award.

_____

4. This veteran Packers cornerback is one of only four football players to win a college championship, a Heisman trophy, and a Super Bowl ring.

_____

5. This Broncos running back's first name is a combination of his dad's nickname (Knowledge) and his mom's first name (Varashon).

_____

6. Through the 2010 season, this Texans receiver ranks first in the NFL in career receiving yards per game (79.7).

_____

7. This Titans running back once ran the 40-yard dash in a blistering 4.24 seconds.

_____

YOUR SCORE

SCORING

Turn to page 79 for the answers. Enter the number you got correct in the box. Once you've finished all the puzzles in the chapter, add up your scores to see how many points you earned in the quarter.

AL TIELEMANS

FOURTH QUARTER SCORE

Write down your scores for each puzzle below and add up the numbers to find out your total.

What's the Call? (p. 64)

Score: _____

Picture Puzzle (p. 67)

Score: _____

M-V-Pieces (p. 70)

Score: _____

Super Bowl Sudoku (p. 65)

Score: _____

Don't Trick Me! (p. 68)

Score: _____

The Scrambler (p. 71)

Score: _____

Word Search (p. 66)

Score: _____

What's in a Name? (p. 69)

Score: _____

Signature Moves (p. 72)

Score: _____

Total:

Extra Point!

See if you can answer this trivia question correctly to convert the extra point. Turn to page 79 for the answer.

In high school, Falcons receiver Roddy White was all-state in football. In which other sport did he win two state titles?

A. Basketball   B. Track and Field
C. Soccer   D. Wrestling

Points from Above: **+** **Extra Point:** **=** **Quarter Total:**

_____   _____

Answers

FIRST QUARTER

PAGE 9
Find the Open Lane

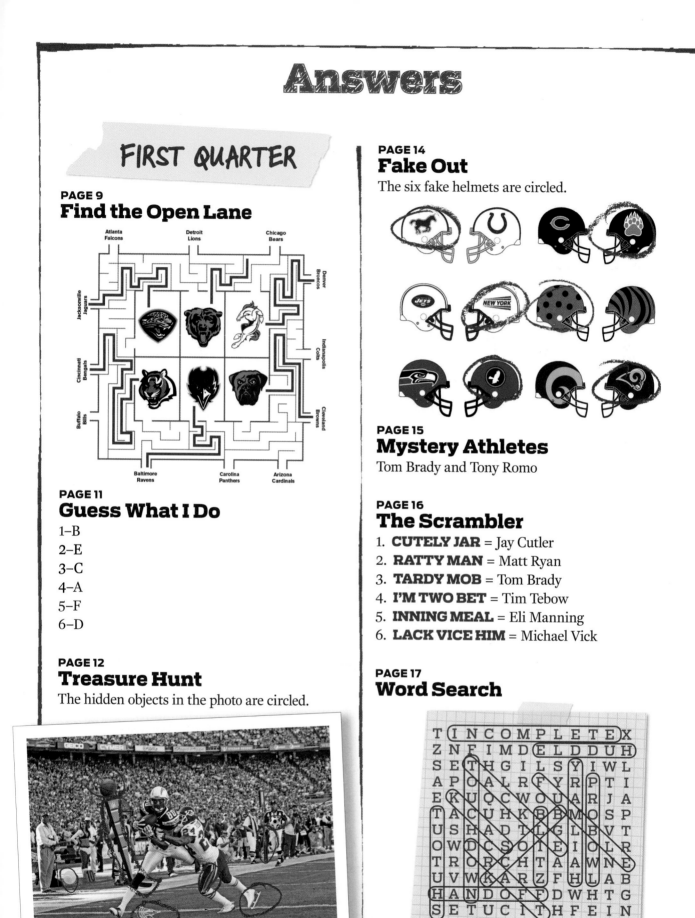

PAGE 11
Guess What I Do

1–B
2–E
3–C
4–A
5–F
6–D

PAGE 12
Treasure Hunt

The hidden objects in the photo are circled.

PAGE 14
Fake Out

The six fake helmets are circled.

PAGE 15
Mystery Athletes

Tom Brady and Tony Romo

PAGE 16
The Scrambler

1. **CUTELY JAR** = Jay Cutler
2. **RATTY MAN** = Matt Ryan
3. **TARDY MOB** = Tom Brady
4. **I'M TWO BET** = Tim Tebow
5. **INNING MEAL** = Eli Manning
6. **LACK VICE HIM** = Michael Vick

PAGE 17
Word Search

Answers

PAGE 18
Scoring Recap
Pittsburgh Steelers 23, Miami Dolphins 22
St. Louis Rams 36, Denver Broncos 33

PAGE 20
That's My Hair

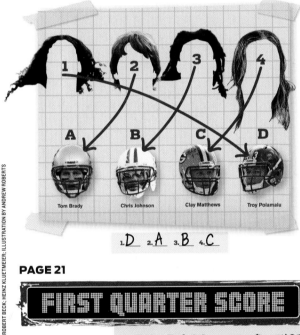

1. D 2. A 3. B 4. C

PAGE 21

FIRST QUARTER SCORE

Extra Point Answer: D. THREE

SECOND QUARTER

PAGE 24
Make the Connection

Answer: TAMPA BAY BUCCANEERS

Start

PAGE 27
Mystery Athletes
Drew Brees and Donovan McNabb

PAGE 28
Gridiron Lingo

1–G	2–C	3–D	4–I	5–E
6–A	7–H	8–F	9–B	

PAGE 30
What's the Call?

1. The Ligers are not allowed to try a field goal. An offensive player may not throw a backward pass out-of-bounds in the final minute of a half. The Ligers are penalized five yards and 10 seconds would be run off the clock, which would end the game.

2. Since Perry never had possession of the ball and the momentum of the kick sent the ball out of the end zone, it is ruled a touchback. The Windmills get the ball at their own 20-yard line.

3. The pass does not count as a completion. A quarterback is not allowed to catch a pass after he has taken a snap from under center, but he can do so from the shotgun formation.

PAGE 31
Letter Lineup

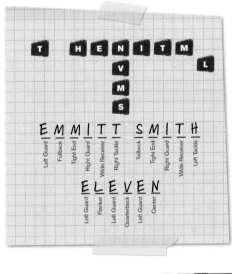

Answers

Brain Teaser
1st place: Shane, punting
2nd place: Phil, kicking
3rd place: Josh, passing

Coach Says
He holds the NFL record for most points scored in a season with 186.

Word Search

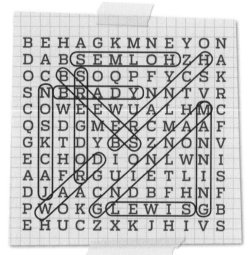

Many Faces of Ochocinco

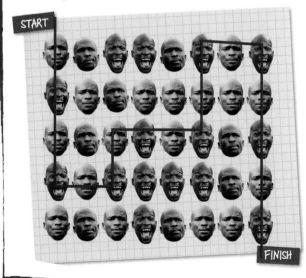

No Place Like Home

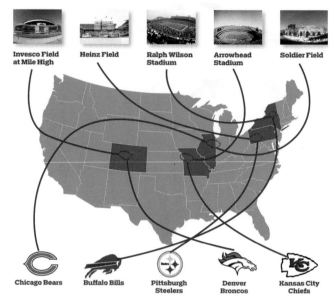

Invesco Field at Mile High · Heinz Field · Ralph Wilson Stadium · Arrowhead Stadium · Soldier Field

Chicago Bears · Buffalo Bills · Pittsburgh Steelers · Denver Broncos · Kansas City Chiefs

Invesco Field at Mile High is located in Colorado and is the home of the Denver Broncos.
Heinz Field is located in Pennsylvania and is the home of the Pittsburgh Steelers.
Ralph Wilson Stadium is located in New York and is the home of the Buffalo Bills.
Arrowhead Stadium is located in Missouri and is the home of the Kansas City Chiefs.
Soldier Field is located in Illinois and is the home of the Chicago Bears.

The Scrambler
1. **JOKE AS SCANNED** = DeSean Jackson
2. **CANNOT MEW** = Cam Newton
3. **ON RAPID EARNEST** = Adrian Peterson
4. **FRIGHTEN WEEDY** = Dwight Freeney
5. **LIZARD TERRY FLAG** = Larry Fitzgerald
6. **TRAINER AS OF** = Arian Foster

SECOND QUARTER SCORE

Extra Point Answer: B. BRETT FAVRE

Answers

THIRD QUARTER

PAGE 42
Word Search

PAGE 44
Rushing Ahead

Hall of Famer _____ Rice	J E R R Y
A coach calls one of these to stop the clock	T I M E O U T
Opposite of a loss in yardage	G A I N
The championship game is the _____ Bowl	S U P E R
A list of 53 players on the team	R O S T E R
Nickname of the Colts' city	I N D Y
To make a touchdown or a field goal	S C O R E
Last pick in the NFL draft is Mr. _____	I R R E L E V A N T
Another word for a victory	W I N

PAGE 46
NFL Comic Code

1. Tom Brady, **E**
2. Anquan Boldin, **H**
3. Aaron Rodgers, **T**
4. Felix Jones, **S**
5. Joe Flacco, **B**
6. Wes Welker, **L**
7. Greg Jennings, **I**
8. BenJarvus Green-Ellis, **N**
9. Ray Rice, **M**
10. Miles Austin, **A**
11. Ryan Grant, **W**
12. Tony Romo, **H**

Answer: HE WAS THE BEST LINEMAN

PAGE 47
Mystery Athletes
Ronde Barber and Eli Manning

PAGE 49
Sign Language

1. Holding
2. Delay of game
3. First down
4. Offside
5. Touchdown
6. False start

PAGE 50
The Scrambler

1. **A RANGERS ODOR** = Aaron Rodgers
2. **BEST HORRIBLE GREEN** = Ben Roethlisberger
3. **AGENT NINNY MOP** = Peyton Manning
4. **SILVER HIP RIP** = Philip Rivers
5. **MATCH AS TUB** = Matt Shaub
6. **TASTED WARMTH OFF** = Matthew Stafford

PAGE 51
Where's My Teammate?

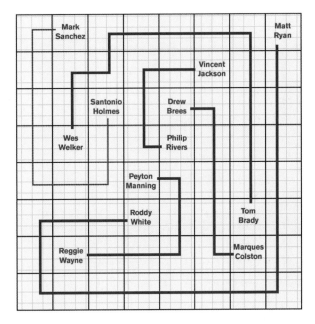

PAGE 52
Athletes in Hiding
Roddy White, DeMarcus Ware, and Cam Newton

Answers

PAGE 53
Picture Puzzle
The eight changes made to the photo are circled.

PAGE 54
Running Back Shuffle
1–Chris Johnson–D   3–Adrian Peterson–B
2–Maurice Jones-Drew–A   4–Ray Rice–C

PAGE 55
Just for Kicks

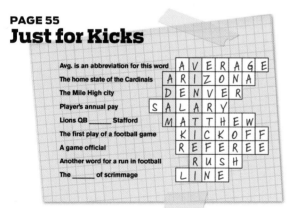

Avg. is an abbreviation for this word	A V E R A G E
The home state of the Cardinals	A R I Z O N A
The Mile High city	D E N V E R
Player's annual pay	S A L A R Y
Lions QB _____ Stafford	M A T T H E W
The first play of a football game	K I C K O F F
A game official	R E F E R E E
Another word for a run in football	R U S H
The _____ of scrimmage	L I N E

PAGE 56
Get the Picture
1. Nose guard   4. Middle linebacker
2. Free safety   5. Wide receiver
3. Long snapper   6. Tailback

PAGE 57

Extra Point Answer: B. SIX

FOURTH QUARTER

PAGE 62
Maze

PAGE 64
What's the Call?
1. The Eagles keep possession. The ball is considered part of Jimenez's body, and he is ruled down by contact as soon as the Suns' player touches the ball.

2. The play is ruled a catch. NFL rules state that officials are considered part of the field of play. The ball is up for grabs.

3. A 15-yard unsportsmanlike conduct penalty is called because coaches are not allowed to be in the white area along the sidelines where officials stand.

PAGE 65
Super Bowl Sudoku

I	V	L	N	S	E	T	G	H
N	E	H	G	V	N	L	S	I
T	G	S	I	H	L	E	V	N
L	S	I	H	T	G	V	N	E
H	N	G	E	I	V	S	T	L
E	T	V	L	N	S	H	I	G
G	L	T	V	E	N	I	H	S
V	H	N	S	L	I	G	E	T
S	I	E	T	G	H	N	L	V

Answer: E L E V E N

Answers

Word Search

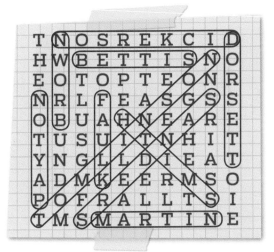

The Answer:

THE TOP TEN
LEAGUE RUSHING
LEADERS OF
ALL TIME

PAGE 67
Picture Puzzle

The eight changes made to the photo are circled.

PAGE 68
Don't Trick Me

1. True
2. False
3. True

4. True
5. True
6. True
7. False

T I M   T E B O W
3 7 2   3 1 6 4 5

PAGE 70
M-V-Pieces

1. Eli Manning
2. Bart Starr
3. Joe Montana
4. Hines Ward
5. Joe Namath
6. Aaron Rodgers
7. Tom Brady
8. Jerry Rice
9. Kurt Warner
10. Drew Brees
11. Emmitt Smith

P E T E   R O Z E L L E
1 2 3 4   5 6 7 8 9 10 11

PAGE 71
The Scrambler

1. **RARE ICY** = Ray Rice
2. **WIN DASHER** = Hines Ward
3. **GREEN LOGS** = Greg Olsen
4. **CHIRPY RAVEN** = Percy Harvin
5. **CZAR HEN MASK** = Mark Sanchez
6. **DESERVE HINT** = Devin Hester

PAGE 72
Signature Moves

1. Adrian Peterson
2. Mario Williams
3. Drew Brees
4. Charles Woodson
5. Knowshon Moreno
6. Andre Johnson
7. Chris Johnson

PAGE 73

FOURTH QUARTER SCORE

Extra Point Answer: D. WRESTLING

GAME OVER!

Great work! Now add up your scores from each quarter and see where you rank.

First Quarter Points: _____

+

Second Quarter Points: _____

+

Third Quarter Points: _____

+

Fourth Quarter Points: _____

=

GRAND TOTAL:

How Did You Do?

Rookie (0–75 points) You showed plenty of promise, and your best football is still ahead of you. Re-try some of the tougher puzzles in the Playbook and see if you can improve your score!

Starter (76–175 points) Nice work. You showed determination and toughness as you worked your way through the Playbook. It doesn't hurt to try some puzzles again, because there are still more yards to be gained!

Pro Bowler (176–250 points) You've proven yourself to be a special talent, showing the skills to move through the Playbook like few others have done. You're a star!

Hall of Famer (251 or more points) A legendary performance! Only a special few reach Hall of Fame level, and the amazing work you've done in the Playbook makes you one of them.

JOHN BIEVER